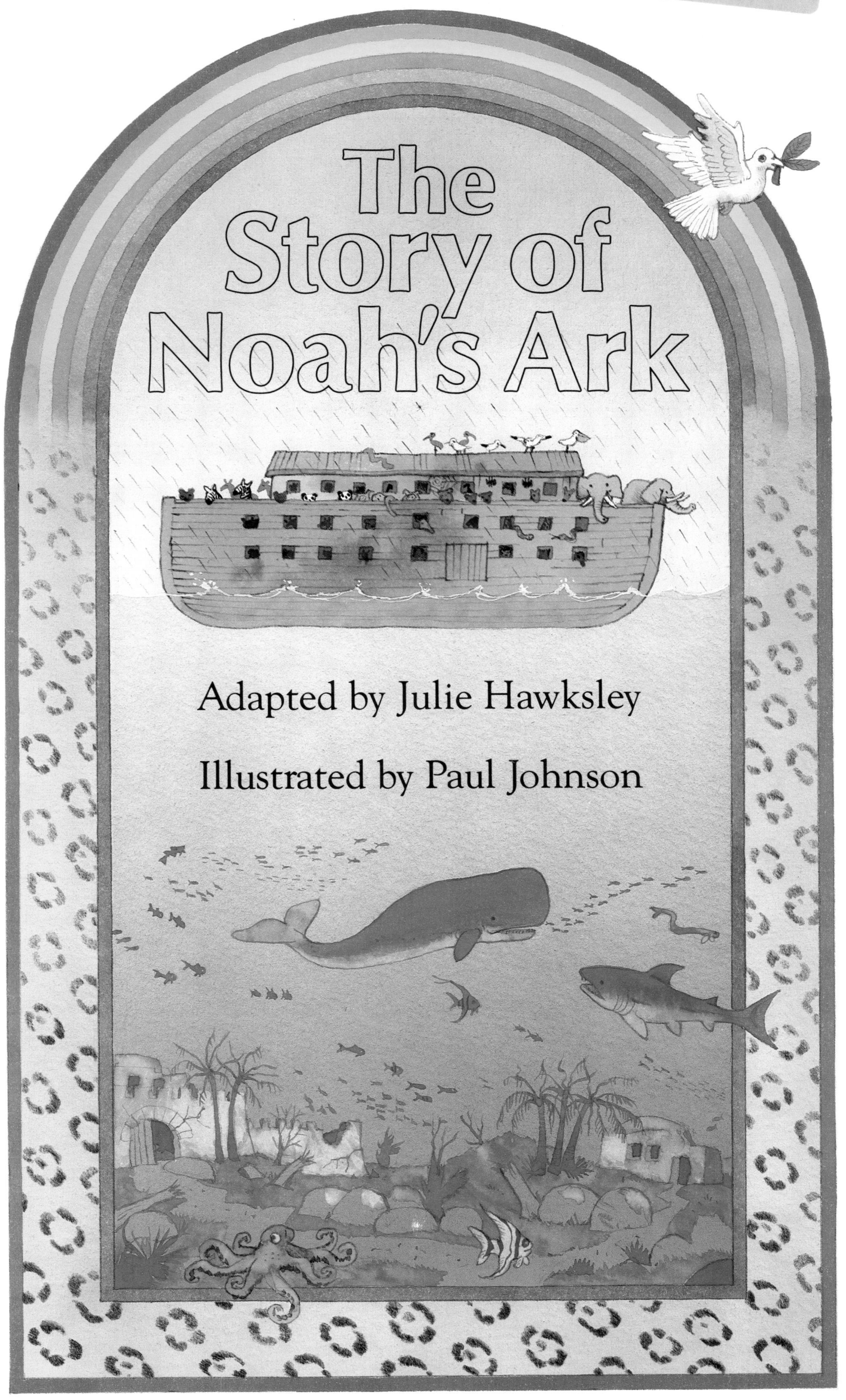

The Story of Noah's Ark

Adapted by Julie Hawksley

Illustrated by Paul Johnson

The Lord was full of sorrow. Everywhere He looked on earth there was violence and unkindness. He was sorry that He had made man, and decided to destroy His creation by causing a great flood to sweep over the world. But there was one good man amongst the bad, by the name of Noah, and the Lord spoke to him.

"Noah," said the Lord, "You must build an ark so that you and your family can escape the flood." He told Noah how to build the ark, and asked him to gather two of each animal and bird and put them on board, so that they might escape the flood, too.

FEATHERSTONE METHODIST SUNDAY SCHOOL
Presented to
Chloe Lamont
First Class
Prize
1989 — 1990
HIGHWAY PUBLISHING
PRINTED IN GREAT BRITAIN

CARNIVAL

Noah listened, and he obeyed the Lord. He set about building the ark as he had been instructed, with the help of his family. He built a huge boat out of cypress wood: with three decks and a roof. When it was done he waterproofed it with pitch, so that it would outlast the flood.

Noah gathered together two of every sort of living creature on earth, except for the animals that lived in water. What a noise there was! What a commotion! Noah led them all into the safety of the ark. Last of all, he told his wife and his sons, Shem, Ham and Joseph and their wives, to get on board. Then Noah himself entered, and the Lord shut the big wooden door tight.

And so they waited inside the ark — Noah and his wife, Noah's sons and their wives, and all the animals. Tiny mice and giant elephants, timid sheep and fierce lions, creeping snakes and proud eagles, they all waited. On the seventh day Noah said "Hush!" and they heard the first drops of rain on the roof. The rain fell harder and harder, until it seemed that a great waterfall would engulf the ark.

The earth cracked open and water gushed out in huge fountains. The sky was as dark as night. Lightning flashed and thunder roared as the waters rose and the ark began to float. All the dry land on earth was covered in water and still it poured. It rained for forty days and forty nights, and all life perished, except for the animals in the water and the animals and people on the ark.

Eventually the rain stopped. But still the earth was covered in water. It remained flooded for one hundred and fifty days, while the ark drifted here and there with no land in sight. But the Lord had not forgotten the ark and its precious cargo. He made a wind blow, and slowly the wind dried the earth. Soon the peaks of mountains could be seen above the water, and on one of these peaks, called Mount Ararat, the ark came to rest.

But the mountain was still just a tiny speck of land in a vast ocean. After another forty days Noah set free a dove to see if its feet could find a dry perch. But the dove came back. It could not find anywhere to rest its feet, and Noah knew that it was not yet safe to let all the animals out of the ark.

After another seven days Noah set the dove free again. And this time it came back with the twig of an olive branch in its beak. So Noah knew the water was going down, but it was still not safe to venture out. After another seven days he set the dove free and this time it did not come back at all. Now Noah knew that the land was dry and safe once more.

Noah released all the animals from the ark. And the Lord spoke to him again, "Never again will I destroy life. This is my promise to you. And if ever you are afraid there will be another great flood when it rains, look up to the sky. There you will see a rainbow, which will be a sign of my promise to you. Now, go forth, and fill the earth with life."